Therapy Poetry
From The Notebook Of A Child Abuse Survivor

©2011 by Clara B. Ray.
All rights reserved. No part of this book may be reproduced, stored in a retrieval system or transmitted in any form or by any means without the prior written permission of the author, except by a reviewer who may quote brief passages in a review to be printed in a newspaper, magazine or journal.

Therapy Poetry By Clara B. Ray
ISBN-13: 978-1466358508
First Printing

Dedication Page

To My Sons Michael & W.C.

Tie the strings on tiny shoes,
Precious moments curling
Tautly to the heart

And later on in latter life,
Just like the wings hinged
To birds in flight

It will be those things,
Which tug these strings
That reign important

Everything else...
Is optional.

07-08-11
Clara B. Ray

About The Author

Website: http://www.clarabpoetry.com
E-mail: clarabpoetry@att.net

Clara B. Ray is a published author who has been writing poetry for about three years. She grew up in rural Ardmore, Oklahoma, as Clara Finley, is 54 years old, and currently resides in Oklahoma City. "Therapy Poetry" is her third book.

Clara gained valuable experience and media exposure as a writer and speaker, while serving as a volunteer victim advocate for the Oklahoma City YWCA Crisis Intervention Center & Battered Women's Shelter.

She is an adult survivor of paternal child abuse, who witnessed her mother endure domestic violence. She cherished being the media relations person present in 1991, as the mayor proclaimed October as Domestic Violence Awareness Month in Oklahoma City. Her writing often reflects these experiences.

Although Clara is a licensed minister, she does not occupy a pulpit at this time, nor does she plan to return to active ministry. She would like to pursue a degree in a writing related field after retiring from over 24 years of employment with the State of Oklahoma.

Part I

Childhood & Teen-age Years

Street corners beckon...
Bargaining, begging for time...
Epilogues vary

08-21-11
Haiku by Clara B. Ray

A Girl. Abused. A Gun.

I was just a little girl,
The first time I heard the footsteps
Walking close to my bed,
With a voice yelling for me to get up--
And when I did---
I felt the cold steel of a shotgun to my head.

I stood there in shock, a little girl thinking
Oh please, won't all of this go away?
I don't want to be here, I want to go outside and play.
Tears on my shirt, rolling down my cheek,
I tried to stop them by blinking.

The biggest hurt, the sharpest pain,
Came from this:
The hand with the gun was supposed to belong
To a robber,
A thief, an unknown rapist.
Somebody who didn't know me.
Instead, I was looking into familiar eyes,
The eyes of my daddy.

For a long time after that,
I tried to be good, thinking
Something had to be wrong with me,
But, it never mattered, how good I had been,
The same thing, soon, would be happening again.

I moved away from home about fifteen years old,
And started a path to get my life back...
Determined that nobody else,

Would tell me to wake up, get up, line up and feel…
The mixture of fear and steel.
I would be my own boss, I alone, would be in control.

I stayed stoned, I stayed lit, I stayed out all night,
A teen alcoholic,
Breaking down and putting the silver
To pounds of marijuana,
And when somebody wanted to buy a lid,
My grown up friends let me deliver it.

My life settled into the ultimate perfection:
The scared little girl disappeared,
And a teen-age me was in charge of all situations.

Yeah. This time around,
I was the daddy. I was in control.
And I knew it. I had my own gun.

02-08-2009
Clara B. Ray

Narrative:

I remember feeling helpless, unable to stop my father, when he tried to shoot us. Nothing I could do at all. That loss of control I felt then, ruled my life, with me putting one band-aid after another on those feelings of no control. My poem shows me finding control the wrong way, a dangerous teen-age life style that could have ended my life. (Continued)

I finally went to church, at 17, and then to therapy later as an adult, to learn the tools necessary to find the right feelings. I validated them, mourned their loss, they released and I no longer felt out of control. I'm glad I learned the right way to cope with leftover pain from abuse in the childhood. Bringing an end to days of an out of control, abused inner child being in control of my current day to day life.

A Small World

A child's hand,
is meant to hold things
chosen by fascinated eyes,
shiny red trucks, kiss-sweetened dolls,
squiggly-wiggly spiders and butterflies.

A child's eyes,
are meant to view a world
of adventure, playgrounds and fun,
snowflakes, rainbows,
amusement parks,
a mother's smiling face,
and a bright shining sun.

A child's feet,
are meant to skip and run,
the heart designed to love,
be loved in return...
Yes! Pure and complete!
A full cycle of affections!

A child's body is meant to be warmed,
clothed, fed, held closely when afraid,
and when sleep fills tiny eyelids,
tucked securely into bed.

Oh how forgiveness within me
seeks to flee,
when a child is beaten, or abused,
neglected or scarred emotionally!

An innocent view of the world,
a view earned by birth,
now forever marred.

This is not the way…
A small world is meant to be.

03-27-10
Clara B. Ray

Ribbons & Bows

She couldn't say a word
When he touched her, in a wrong spot,
And a little hurt became a lot.

She didn't say a word,
She didn't dare...

Her tears allowed themselves
Hours later,
Because her ribbon wouldn't tie straight,
In her hair.

03-27-09
Clara B. Ray

A Child, A River, A Mountain, A Wall

How wide
Be the river,
Yea? Nay? Sufficiency thereof,
For an abused child to hide?
A river
How wide?

How tall
Be the mountain?
Are inches found,
To gather flung concerns?
Can height conceal, of them, some?
Perhaps, in these then, its metric meters,
A child can place them all,
A mountain
How tall?

Sigh. In oft analysis to a poet's astonishment,
An abused child answers his own call,
Saying... Strong support system found...
My back against a wall.

03-15-09
Clara B. Ray

A Mask Goes Up In Smoke

Wildflower...
what you doing out
with these hardheads
this time of hour?

Question heard often
by me at fifteen.
I hit the reefer joint...
drug-drawled my answer again...
just getting my head right, Man.

Mask of street
straight-up
going up
with each toke
of smoke.

Spirit intruded by the pain of abuse
soul calling, searching for a truce.

Tell somebody? Tried that.
Call the cops? Done that.
Didn't work ya'll.
What's the use?

So, night after night,
on hidden fears, tears,
hard liquor and marijuana
I did choke...

A street-bad stance
covering the pain,
my mask going up
and on
in smoke.

11-01-2008
Clara B. Ray

The Same Shit My Daddy Drinks

Fresh from the country
Sipping 7-up and gin
I was chilling in the clubs...
Daddy & his shotgun now a has-been.

No passing the bottle for me
I was 15 and drinking proper,
Waitress-delivered,
One shot for a dollar and quarter.

Self-esteem seemed to be at an all time high
My daddy's rejection kissed good-bye,
Cute guys were checking me out,
I was hearing the words... "Oh baby you so fine"
Words I needed to hear a lot.

High-fiving, Shooting the Power,
I thought for sho' I had arrived,
Yeah, this was my hour.

In just a few I found a friend,
And I was so in love with that young man,
He started paying for the 7-UP & gin,
And when my taste switched to Coke and Rum,
He just snapped his finger, called a waitress,
And bought his girl some.

He was 17 and fine
I was his
And he was mine.

My heart and three things only
He told me he needed from me...
To be his woman, carry his gun,
And know how to run, if he needed a gun...
And didn't have one.

Over looking the G in He,
We were together two sweet years, inseparably.
Then Slick split to get a job, a year out of school,
For un-employment ceased its cool.

I was alone, lonely, and melancholy
I was 17 and didn't have nobody,
I told Slick's friends to keep the reefer,
Give me a glass and pass the bottle. I was cold.
I needed to drink to warm my soul.

Today it's plain to see
My child abused butt needed therapy,
As my proper drinking days of gin & rum soon left me,
And I was filling my glass with big boy brew...
Thunderbird, Gallo, Morgan David aka:
Mad Dog Twenty-Twenty.

And in disbelief, a teen-age me, learned the depths
An alcoholic & its bottle soon sink...

When I cried out loud in the club,
Somebody please help me, this can't be...
I'm drinking the same shit my Daddy drinks.

12-16-2008
Clara B. Ray

When A Child Cries

When a child cries,
may there be
someone there
to wipe weary tears
from tiny
weeping
eyes.

When a child cries,
may he never realize
fountains
flowing
down
upon
a
small
face,
feeling as if...
they are in the right place.

When. Where.
An abused child cries.

05-27-2010
Clara B. Ray

Sometimes Even Big Boys Cry

Sometimes,
Even big boys cry.

Amid distant stares,
Discouraging masculinity's opened skies,
Mature male eyes relinquish liquid memories.

The taste of their salinity traced to violence,
Heart ache, heart break and abuse,
Supposed unique
To feminine gender, only.

Sigh. For in the reality of life,
Excepted of child birth and menses flow,
All other pain, discrimination, victimization,
Abuse, harassment, and inequality--
Inclusively, a man might also know.

And of abuse to a child,
The same things that happen to little girls,
Happen to little boys too,
Yes they do.

And sometimes, pain from the same,
Primes the lacrimal glands even of a man,
And become the reasons why,
That sometimes,
Even big boys cry.

02-11-2010
Clara B. Ray

A Short Story: Soon One Morning

It was a hot Sunday morning in a southern Oklahoma country church. My face stuck to the fan as I tried to keep both the sweat and the flies from clinging to my skin.

I saw Mama give me a stern look whenever I put the wooden stick of the fan into my mouth and chewed on it. I was really wondering: How could she sit there quietly in church, and expect me to do the same, after what had happened last night? It was the first time Daddy came home in a drunken rage, awakened us children, and made us line up in the living room, with his loaded shotgun cocked and aimed at us, walking slowly from one to the other, trying to decide if we would be shot.

As these thoughts were running through my mind, the un-carpeted wood floors of the church echoed a somber song into my heart. The stiletto high heels of women's shoes clicking each note deeper and deeper into my soul. It was the mid 1960's and the church was singing… "Soon one morning death come a-creeping at my door… Soon one morning death come a-creeping at my door… Oh my Lord, oh my Lord what shall I do?"

It was then I understood that to children being abused-- sometimes death, pain, hurt, & abuse comes in a Daddy's khaki pants, and his straw looking, brown, canvas-soled shoes. (Continued)

There are 4 children who die in America each day, from child abuse or neglect. For those children-- the acapella song of a small country church still plays on.

01-09-2011
Clara B. Ray

Blue Ribbon Winners

Days dawn grey for the child abused,
The sun shines
With pessimistic colored disposition,
Questions of a painless day
Answered nay, by reality
Responding to a relief-seeking conscience.

The ride to school with sleep-laden eyes,
Ears hinging to audio
Streaming envied lists of
Other kid's problems,
A face with a pimple, cheeks without
The latest 'Girl Doll' dimple.
The abused child daydreams for
Vexation so simple!

Time fast forwards to adult life,
A husband. A wife. Children.
And the choice to be a continued sinner,
Or a loving, non-abusive parent...
A Blue Ribbon winner.

Halting the horrifics of hurt to a child,
Emotionally stinging, physically crippling,
Sexually vile.

Yea! A blue ribbon, worn down to the soul!
And to the continuation of abuse,
We say Nay. We end the cycle.
We shut the door.

And the hurt we suffered as a child,
Hurts a child no more. Applause. Bravo.
Encore.

01-17-10
Clara B. Ray

Part II

The Young Adult Years

My heart searched.
My heart found.
Then,
My heart heard a call to search again.

Until my heart understood, at last...
It searched not for the future,
It searched,
For the child abuse I suffered in the past.

01-16-2011
Clara B. Ray

All Roads Led...

Twisting, turning, 360 spins,
Dead-ending and curving.

Mile after searching mile,
All roads, for inner reconciliation,
From a father's alcoholic rage, abuse
And vexation...

Yes, all roads led,
to
my
abused
inner
child.

09-05-2010
Clara B. Ray

Steeples of Sincerity

Daily a heart implored of God,
Silent litanies steeped in sincerity.

The visible peripherals
Sought
In return
Thought
To be essential
As propitious tokens
Indicative of
A domiciled spirituality
Enclosed within.

Decades later,
Days cloaked in quasi-pious existence,
A precious lesson, an assayed heart learned.

When thoughts of a need for therapy
Are really God tugging at the heart,
And all that is being done--
Is beseeching the Ens Entium One...

This may not be enough
To silence
A querulous cacophony
Of an earthly father's rejection.

06-20-2010
Clara B. Ray

Narrative: Steeples of Sincerity

I am an adult survivor of child abuse, and although I was warned it would not be enough, I thought that a religious conversion was all that I needed forever, and ever and ever. I was wrong, I needed the inclusion of therapy for the abuse I suffered in my childhood.

I have many friends of many faiths, and some of no faith at all. It does not matter the faith, or the methods, whether meditating, yoga, or prayer to my Higher Power, God Jehovah & his son- Jesus Christ. It is often not enough, alone, to find the level of inner peace needed to silence the pain of rejection and/or abuse by mothers, fathers, or other adult authority figures.

Also, the search for abused inner child feelings will often cause an obsession with that faith/belief as a substitute, as we seek for the relief of release.

In my case, a life of drugs, guns & thugs was replaced with a life of only prayer & church, literally 24 hours a day and almost 7 days a week. A better and safer lifestyle, yes, but the root problem of unresolved inner child issues remained firmly in place.

For adults who were abused as children, a combination of the two, faith and therapy has proven to be the right choice for many.

Wine Stains

Tic-Toc!
So
precious
the time--
seized from hands
of yesterday's clock!

Years
of pater's
drunken rage
refusing removal
from
life's
center stage.

Daughters of time,
were they all!
Impregnated
with seconds
stolen
from
earlier
moments of mine.

Long was the labor in therapy!
But, longest was the afterwards rest,
in antiqued minutes returned to me.

Time tediously squeezed
from a childhood bruised,
in scars, abuse and memories.

Where no in between comforts remained,
and life was split into units
of either plain or psychedelic,
nice mother or father insane.

Of love or hate,
boiled or frozen, too early or too late.

Of evil or angel,
rejected or chosen, circles or angles.

Oh the wars and vexation,
of abstinence or over-indulgence,
and how a heart longed,
to know the placidity of moderation!

However, in the end,
the middle of the road was found again.

And a woman understood,
from whence the extremes came.

And, understanding
the abrupt change of scenes
in a childhood,
permitted the removal,
of an alcoholic father's…
violent, violet wine stains.

07-04-2010
Clara B. Ray

A Child, Sunglasses & A Mystery

I like to wear sunglasses
So you can't see,
What I can not tell you...
That somebody is abusing me.

When I get grown,
And the abuse has ceased to be,
I still won't leave home...
Without my sunglasses on.

02-22-2009
Clara B. Ray

She Was Cold: Part I

She was cold.
His arms were warm.
As heat from affection
Was absent from home,
She used his arms in warm substitution.

She felt the heat of his breath, around her face
As he whispered his want into her hair.

His desire traced circles around her ear,
And something inside--
Yearned for more of its warmth,
As to her bosom, his lips came near.

Their bodies immersed,
Their heat became one,
Then,
He was gone.

His masculine scent upon the covers she clutched,
Did not yield any sparks
Of much needed acceptance,
For the chill still shuddering in her soul.

She cries, and hopes he returns,
For she is still cold.

01-30-2009
Clara B. Ray

Narrative: She Was Cold: Warmth of Self-Acceptance

The abuse of a child is also an act of rejection. This rejection is a cold reality for a child, and one never forgotten. Its chill remains in our psyche or inner child, until the child is accepted by the authority figure.

If this acceptance is never provided by the parent or authority figure, the adult survivor of that abuse must then provide this acceptance and the warmth it brings to those feelings of coldness. The "search" for a substitute can be long, cruel, and often just as abusive as the childhood abuse.

This poem and the next 4 poems are a series called: "She Was Cold". It speaks of this search for the warmth and glow of self-acceptance.

It's too late for our parents or authority figures to provide us with this warmth of acceptance. We must mourn that lost, and then give ourselves and our inner child, this much needed acceptance. We deserve it!

Yes, learn to parent your own inner child. Know the glow of self-acceptance, and bring your inner child out of the cold!

She Was Cold Part II: Fur Coats

She was still cold.
Even with her sunglasses on.

Her inner child chill, was not warmed,
By the substitution of a man's arms,
So she bought a fur coat,
To cover her chill,
And with that, she felt she could now be warm...
At will.

She luxuriated,
In the luxury of its opulence,
Surrounding herself with its mink,
An exhilarating substitute, it seemed,
For everything she lacked,
Including, subconsciously, even a father's acceptance.

The heat doesn't reach her inner child,
But for now, it was enough.

And if not...
She thought...
I can always go out,
And buy... more, and more and more... stuff.

02-23-2009
Clara B. Ray

She Was Cold Part III: Food

She was cold. Again.
A mink coat's opulence soon lost its newness,
And her abused inner child, cried inside,
For the warmth of self-acceptance.

More efforts without,
To pacify the pain within,
Did indeed begin, again.

Deliciously and selectively,
With foods of rich succulence,
She provides for the coldness,
Of an inner child, abused and anonymous.

And, oh! The comfort,
The extravagance! The abundance!
The warmth of a succulent food's succulence!

For the abused inner child within her,
Insufficient it was, as acceptance and love,
But for now, for her, it was enough.
Aye. Rich! Sweet! Savory! Sapid! Nectarous!
She smiles a familiar smile.

And with resplendent cuisines,
She feels the deceptive satisfaction, uncovered,
When the substitute for self-acceptance...
Is food as comfort.

02-24-2009
Clara B. Ray

She Was Cold Part IV: Weight Gain

Finally, a victorious warmth.
Her over-indulgence in foods of sumptuous succulence,
Provided extra layers of skin. She could feel its heat,
And wore the added pounds like a coveted garment.

Her sub-conscious
Turns up the corners of her mouth into a happy smile,
For, the warmth she missed as an abused child,
At last... its chill... she could not feel.

And with the weight, a plan she could follow,
To fill the sunken spots inside, so cold and so hollow...
She would keep the extra layers of skin,
And she would never be cold again.

Her face glows with the radiance of its heat.
A glorious warmth enveloped her.
Completely. From top to bottom. All around.
Her whole body…
A soothing heat, does surround.

As before, the pounds can't reach her inner child,
And the child within... remains abused & anonymous.
But for her, for now, it is enough.

She felt good.
She displayed a new confidence.
And it looked good.

The weight was valuable to her,
And she clothed her value appropriately
In designer chemise silhouette dresses.
And, she accented her gain,
With well-deserved, well-coiffed tresses.

And when her inner child,
Cried for the warmth of acceptance,
She could now offer a better pacifier,
Volumes of weight and its warmth,
As a substitute, for security and for comfort.

02-25-09
Clara B. Ray

She Was Cold Part V: Warm At Last!

Shivers. Chill bumps. Covering layers of flesh,
Volumes of fat. She was cold again.

A pained groan escapes from within,
As the coldness returns,
And her abused inner child yearns,
For the warmth of self-acceptance.

In solitude...
A multitude...
Of reflections. Of recollections.
A soul-searching examination and realization.

Self-gratifying substitutes
For a father's acceptance,
For a mother's warmth,
Will not. Does not. And can not, constitute...
A very necessary inner self-affection.

She has no more options of places to flee,
So she gathers her thoughts,
And sojourns in the coldness of therapy
And memories.

She wanders through years of substitutions
Until she reaches her own spirit,
And for the first time,
She feels an old pain within it.

A desperate, anguished cry, springs
From her inner most being,
It sparks a memory of lost feelings.
A spark of heat. At last! A tiny bit of heat!

Her mind lunges towards the warmth,
Reaching for its heat.
Breaking through the thick darkness
Of suppressed memories,
She finds it, and ends an anonymity.

For there she is,
Seen now only in a memory...
A frightened little girl,
With exactly the same desperate anguished cry,
Springing
From her being.

Suddenly, quietly,
For that brave little girl she had been,
Hurt, abused, rejected and broken.
A warmth of compassion fills her. Completely.
And, she is warm with self-acceptance.

With self-acceptance fueling her confidence,
The world takes on a new look.
It is an azure expanse of wide open sky.
She spreads her wings gracefully,
Ready now to fly.

02-26-09
Clara B. Ray

The Race To Recovery

Lean forward,
In the race to recovery

Try to feel,
The tape across your chest

For, of all the people, to mend a tiny heart,
Torn apart…
By the abuse of another,
You can do it best.

09-24-11
Clara B. Ray

Narrative: The Race To Recovery

As an adult survivor of child abuse, a prior audience member viewing domestic violence, I feel triumphant. I have reached an understanding of what happened to the emotions I felt, and those I was blessed not to feel, as a child trying to grasp, bear, understand my Father and his shotgun aimed at me over, and over again.

It was not an easy journey, and I can not claim to have been a perfect traveler. I can't boast of having been a well-behaved student of "inner-revelations". But, I can say that I made it. (Continued)

I can't say I haven't made mistakes, I can't say my teenage years didn't include behavioral problems. I can't say they were drug-free. I can't say they were alcohol-free. No, I can't say that.

I can't say I didn't learn new math: Kilos, Pounds, Lids. New Gym Class: Walking from one side of town to the other delivering drugs, guns.

New Colors: Purple Haze, Yellow Sunshine. What size purse to carry in a club: One big enough for a .22, .38 or Sawed-Off, all property of my new older friends, depending on how much trouble they had caused beforehand.

I can't say, throughout my search for 'Acceptance', that my family put a stamp of approval, on all my friends, and they were all my age. No, I can't say that. I seem to remember the words gangsters, hoodlums and thugs.

I can't say that as an adult, when those abused child feelings stirred in my spirit, that I didn't act out, blurt out, melt down, cry out or show out, trying to reach them, find them, touch them, satisfy them. No, I can't say that.

But, I can say, strengthened by My Higher Power, God, I kept searching... through years of therapy. I leaned to feel the tape of recovery, across my chest, and I made it. (Continued)

Finding the me that was in pain, hurting, confused, searching for her Daddy that loved her. I found her-- and I was no longer lost in my search. I examined those feelings, of me at that age, accepted them-- and no longer felt a need for acceptance from anybody, or anywhere else.

I understood it was not Clara, at 54, that was or is in need. It was Clara at 7, 9, 11, standing there with Daddy, with his shotgun in his hand, at her head.

I validated my feelings of it all, though not all at once, it took about 10 years. Then I felt their release, and concluded my search. I ended my journey. My spirit smiled: triumphant!

It is my hope and prayer that all adult survivors of child abuse, domestic violence, be blessed to do the same.

Co-Dependency: Missing Parts

To compliment the other, to complete another,
In relationships, in companionship,
A difference befalls the twain.

The first needing be done, infinitely,
And of the latter, sometimes 'tis wise to refrain.

For to compliment is to flavor,
And of this, it is good to savor.

However, to complete another, wherever, whenever,
The other lacks wholeness, and has a missing of parts,
In my opinion… works seldom to never.

For each person must reach inside their own hearts…
To find their own missing parts.

02-22-10
Clara B. Ray

Narrative:

Life has its moments, for all of us. Some moments are more difficult for the adult child abuse survivor. One of these moments occurs when another person has an inner child need, and clings to us fill that need, or as my poem stated, be that missing part. How tempting it is to our unfulfilled childhood needs, to be needed! Sadly, we must face a harsh reality: Each person must take a stroll through their hearts, and find their own missing parts. Co-dependency is not healthy.

I Write A Book

Dismal commune
of heart and soul
beckoned me,
a call for peering inwardly,
and honestly.

For backwards walking
through days and years,
shining lights into dark places,
openly confronting daunting fears.

With each step that I took,
bits and pieces of me
dribbled
down
and around,
surrounding my footprints,
in
sweetly
salted
tears.

I walked forward then, gathering the fragments,
Saying nay to tossing them away,
Scribbling them into poetry.

Yes. Soft pages. Within a hardcover book.
My calligraphy.

04-01-11
Clara B. Ray

Part III

Domestic Violence:
Understanding My Mother's Pain

It is not good for mothers to cry,
For tiny hands,
Can not wipe the tears,
From her soul or eyes.

Oh weep not, Mater!
For tiny hands
Can not
Cease the waters,

Nor can little minds understand... why?
No. It is not good for mothers to cry.

10-03-2010
Clara B. Ray

The Sound of Domestic Violence

Sister, Sister, of bowed head, broken spirit,
My mother's voice cries to me, silently
From scattered, jagged pieces of your soul.

Sister, Sister, of eyes anonymous,
My mother's voice cries to me-
When one suffering abuse walks among us,
Without regard to the color of skin,
Worn upon the body, that she who is beaten
Is enclosed within.

For Black is beautiful, aye, this is true,
But we are all the same color
When the black is a shade of 'Deeply Bruised' blue,
And blond hair shining golden upon the head,
Is highlighted in colors of 'Your Own Blood' red.

Oh my Sister, Sister, of bowed head, broken spirit,
My mother's voice, filled with doubt,
Thrown at her to douse confidence,
Above that which an angry man's berating instills,
Speaks quietly to me--

Bruised parts of your heart, saying,
Have you a balm that heals?
Sister. Sister.

06-06-2010
Clara B. Ray

A Short Story: Mama Goes To Therapy

Chapter I

It was a warm, quiet Christmas Day. The weather was so mild, December felt like Spring. I was enjoying the holiday with Mama and my sisters, the familial atmosphere cordial, comfortable. And then, the traditional family game time began, and the cordial air gave way to serious faces.

One of my sisters opened up a new game. It was some kind of psychological trivia. She began to confront my mother as to why she had not left Dad, as he had been extremely abusive to her and to us, his children.

"Why didn't you just leave, Mama? Daddy tried to kill us all with that shotgun. He kept hurting you, yelling, screaming, drunk all the time, cutting you with his pocketknife. He kicked you, with the baby in one hand and that shotgun in the other.

As adults we are all in therapy, our lives are reeling from that bullshit that Daddy did to us and you. Why didn't you leave, Mama? Why didn't you just leave?"

Chapter II

"I didn't know I could", my mother replied. "I really thought I didn't have no place to go. Your baby sisters already asked me to come to therapy with them, (Continued) for some of that confrontational psychology. I went and I'm glad, because I learned something I didn't know: A woman got options. And I am so sorry I didn't know this earlier. A woman got options."

"I didn't know a woman could leave. I didn't know I had that option, as the therapist called it. I was born a Black woman in 1923, have only a 4th grade education. In my days women got married, took care of the house and kids, and stayed with their husbands. If he did something wrong, the Law decided his punishment."

"I called the sheriff on him each time, they picked him up, and brought him back home, never charging him with anything. Nobody told me that I could leave. Until I went to therapy with your sisters, I never knew it was a possibility. There were no shelters and support groups back then. I felt like I had no place to go."

"And I just learned what I should have known years ago... A woman can leave a mean husband. A woman got options."

Chapter III

Hmmm ... not much for me to add is it? Other than to say that this applies to both men & women in abusive relationships. And, it is even more important to those adults who were also abused as children. We need to know that now --as adults-- we have options. Options that were not available to us as children being abused. (Continued)

If this idea is not available to us emotionally, I think we need to do what my Mama did... go to therapy, until we, as adult survivors of child abuse can understand... 'leaving the abusive relationship as an option'. Sometimes, understanding this as an option, while it is an option, can be hard for those of us who are child abuse survivors. I understand this. And hope and pray that this enlightenment arrives while there is still time to leave.

I was blessed to never be a victim of spousal abuse. But, I am still glad to have heard my mother say it. This was worth its weight in gold to me, and shall never be forgotten. Leaving an abusive situation is an option for adults. Yes. Options. I like that word. A woman got options.

Epilogue ~

I didn't know what it was at that time, but, I remember my inner child smiling that day.

And, it came many years later, but I finally understood that what happened to my mother was an abuse called domestic violence. I spent time in classes, workshops and therapy, learning all I could about it. I needed to make peace with my mother's pain. Understanding the dynamics of domestic violence capacitated me to do so.

Rest in peace, Mama.

The Abused Woman Is A Flower

The flower blooms.
Its petals open slowly,
And, a colorful, strong,
Fragrant beauty unfolds.

It is receptive and responds
To light, touch, moisture
A kind voice and pleasant sounds,
But, it receives none.

And tho' highly sought,
Conditions conducive to growth
Are never found.

For the abused woman is this flower,
Nourished by slaps to the face…
As touch.

By the darkness of unconsciousness,
When slaps become blows-- as light,
Her tears and blood for moisture.

Nourished by a voice yelling...
The books you read are dumb,
The clothes you wear are ugly,
You're ignorant. You're stupid!

You can't do anything without me!
Your food tastes like shit. You idiot!

And so nourished, as it bloomed...
WOMAN ABUSED
Slowly folds its petals.

Closing its beauty, strength...
And fragrance from view.

Falling in two steps behind the voice...
Desperately trying to change its words.

10-18-2008
Clara B. Ray

Dedicated to the many women & men in abusive relationships, and in memory of those who didn't survive.

A Short Story: Chalk Up One For God

Chapter I ~

I had traveled this road a thousand times, and knew the hills and curves by heart. The only change was the firm, gritty black top replacing the dusty roads of my childhood. My husband (now ex-husband) and young son enjoyed the gentle ride, magnificent-- with lush spring greenery painting the landscape. Familiar white clouds, and a warm, smiling sun completed the picturesque scene.

We chatted happily as we cruised the last curve and made our way over the final hill, rolling down its rural slope, turning up into the driveway.

And there the beauty stopped. My dad was in the yard with his shotgun, loaded and aimed at my mother, his hand on the trigger.

A million feelings of dread, fear, and sadness filled my heart, as my husband took the gun from Dad, and we continued into the house. My husband was a minister and began to ask my father why he did this. Dad said he was drunk, not in his right mind, had been doing it for years, and this was just the way he was.

Gary said, "Can I pray for you? I know Clara and her family have done all they can, and you were doing this when she was a little girl, she comes home and you are doing it again. I know what to do when nothing
(Continued)

else can be done, I give it to the Lord." A simple prayer was said. Dad said he was sleepy, and went to bed, remaining there asleep for the remainder of the visit.

Chapter II ~

The cheerful yellow color of fresh curtains, blowing gaily in a summer breeze, matched the atmosphere in the living room a year later when I finally made another visit home. I walked toward the stove to get Mama a cup of coffee and Dad said to Mama, "That's all right, Lucille. I will get it for you. I'm standing right next to it". I stood in shock hearing these words spoken to my mother. It was the first time in my almost thirty years of living that I had heard Dad speak to Mama in this tone, offering to do something for her.

Dad continued talking, speaking now to my husband, "Reverend, your prayer worked. I have not picked up my shotgun at my wife and family, I have not had one drink of wine, and I have not tried to cut, push or hit Lucille since that day." My mother confirmed saying Dad been a whole different man since that day that Gary prayed for him. "I live in peace in my own house now."

Dad then said, "I have apologized to my wife, and I don't act or think that way anymore. Clara, if you and my children can forgive me and learn to make it with all the bad memories of what I did, then we can move on."

Chapter III ~

I have not lied in telling my story, and I will not start now by telling you that I answered immediately. Many dark memories of this man flooded my mind. I could still feel the cold steel of his shotgun on my head.

I remembered a dark, violent night when Daddy started to attack my two younger sisters and myself with his pocket knife, after he cut Mama. I didn't forget the bright red blood streaming from her arm. I told him as he came into our room, "You better keep doing that to Mama. You don't have the shotgun tonight and I'm not scared of your knife. I got my own." I pulled my blade and told him, "One step into our room and I will cut your throat. As drunk as you are, I know I can win. No man is going to do this to me". My father and I stared at each other for a very long minute, and he backed off. I was only about 13 or 14 years old then, but the violence of that night still ran fresh in my adult mind.

Then I looked at Mama. I saw her sitting there in peace, without the shotgun, the knives, the harsh words. I felt the bright peace within the house. I saw this woman that I loved so much, now able to enjoy life, and my decision was made. I would not take this from her. I finally moved out of the door, went to Mama and kissed her. "I'm so happy this has happened, Mama. This is the life I want for you".

I walked over to Dad and did something I had not done in all my life. (Continued)

Kissing him on his cheek, I said, "Daddy, I'm proud of you". As year after year passed, I went home to this same peaceful scene, with Dad not ever returning to his violent abuse. And, until the day Dad died in July of 1987 (with Mama leaving us on New Year's Day 2009), I left again and again saying the same thing to my husband... "Chalk up one for God".

Epilogue ~

I left my childhood home that day knowing I had the responsibility of validating and overcoming the harshness of my abused childhood. My Dad and Mother had done all they could to make the pains of a past abuse right. I was an adult, and it was now my journey to find peace, reconciliation and coping mechanisms for left over pain. It is this journey I write of in my poetry and blogs.

And, this ending, of divine intervention, is also the reason I include divinity poetry in the types of poems I write. In my second book of poetry, "Divinity Poetry By Clara B. Ray", I wanted to honor God for bringing an end to a violent, long term abuse that my family endured.

This ending is not the ending for all women or men suffering abuse. And, I did not add this short story to my poetry for women or men to stay in abusive relationships 'praying for the Lord to fix it'. I admit to (Continued) having mixed emotions about how it ended, as this ending did not include the therapy and education on violence in the home, usually needed to end abuse.

I have conflicting emotions also because, I still needed therapy for the abuse Dad did to me, the physical, sexual and the emotional. His apology did not negate my leftover pain from his abuse, nor did it negate my need for long term, heart wrenching therapy.

But, I am penning the truth as it happened to me. And I have to give the big man, the man upstairs, credit for the peace that finally ruled my childhood home. Yes. Chalk Up One For God.

11-11-2010
Clara B. Ray

Part IV

The Present: Here & Now

Child abuse. We survived.
As adults, many of us are grateful to be alive.

Today,
When
We
Look
Into
The
Mirror
Inwardly...

May we all try hard to see,
That which could not and can not be
Taken away from you or me...
Dignity. Grace. Strength. Beauty.

10-31-2010
Clara B. Ray

For Adult Survivors of Child Abuse

There is a place
Where
The
Mortally
Wounded
Can
Transcend.

Where we can hold
Inner child fears,
Old intimidating feelings,
Tightly
In our hands.

We can know what they are,
We really can understand...

Yes. There is a place
Where
The
Mortally
Wounded
Can
Transcend.

Embrace
Therapy.

03-18-11
Clara B. Ray

Old Wounds, Fresh Salt

Old wounds rubbed
with fresh salt...
child abuse survivors
urged not to talk.

Scars of pain
livid again
under
the dirt
of other's
words...

Talk about it? No. I don't think you should do so,
You really should feel too much shame.

I beg to differ.
We are not the abuser.
We are not the wrong doer.
We are not the ones to bear the blame.

And,
the sunlight of right,
shines bright,
upon
the
child's
face.

05-18-11
Clara B. Ray

Vista Views

Experience rendered the poet reflective,
A heightened conscience awakened,
With a vista view of life
Yea, a new perspective.

Nay to life by quantity,
Aye to life by quality,
And of wars in which to embroil the soul,
A wiser poet is much more selective.

Ended now a constant mull...
The poet's glass is now half-full!

01-12-2010
Clara B. Ray

All Roads Led Part II

At this time in life,
It is quite common to reflect.
On journeys taken. On steps made.

Thoughts of gratitude,
Mix with regret
Over an inner child search, and a high price,
Often paid.

Steps.
Some proud.   Some puzzling.
Some unforgettable. Some regretted.
Some uncomfortable.

In the end, a profitable journey it has been,
The good, the bad, the ugly.

For all steps helped--
To make me who I am today.

And, I am who and what I want to be, finally.
It took mile after searching mile,
But I am now the proud parent of my own inner child.

Yes, a profitable journey it has been,
And of the regrets? Imperfections?
It is what it is my friends.

09-13-10
Clara B. Ray

I Dance The Child

It took a lot longer than a minute,
But therapy was finally finished.
And, a knowledge of the dynamics
Within abused childhoods I had finally gained.

Gone were the re-created & acted out feelings,
The surreal menageries of a little girl's pain,
Paraded like a long funeral processional.
Post therapy demeanor?
Resumed astute professional.

Gone were the thoughts
That it was a tribulation of the soul,
A test of faith, a fiery trial
And a new confidence I now displayed
In knowing it to have been...
The successful search for a lost inner child.

The tears in therapy. The intrusions of memory.
Years wading through feelings of gun's steel...
To head,
Of remembering a little girl's prayers:
My father is alive Lord. Please make him dead.

My teen-age years all sorted out,
I understood why I lived like I was 21,
Out in the clubs, straight-up street and grown,
Breaking down kilos & pounds of reefer before school,
A teen-age alcoholic, helping the guys get their drug
Hustle on.

Now, the strength of my survival,
And a bright future ahead,
Have become my main reflections,
For I have grown to understand
How much more I am, than...
A mentally ill man's sad, sick rejection.

And, although the lessons are now learned,
And I have concluded my search,
With negatives now a past lifestyle,
I shall never forget the scared little girl I was.
I shall never forget how strong I was to endure.

And I shall salute that brave, little girl who stood there,
All lined up with her brothers & sisters,
With Daddy's shotgun, at her head,
Yes, I will acknowledge her, every once in a while.

For in the world of the Written Arts...
Poetry,
Creative Writing,
Public Relations,
Spokesperson,
Performance...

I shall write,
I shall rhyme,
I shall perform,
The passion, the action, the energy of that child.
Yea and Amen. As a writer... I dance the child.

01-08-11
Clara B. Ray

CPSIA information can be obtained at www.ICGtesting.com
Printed in the USA
LVOW080208281011

252461LV00001B/82/P